Your Body At Work

How Your Eyes Work

by Carol Ballard

Gareth Stevens
Publishing

Please visit our Web site, www.garethstevens.com.
For a free color catalog of all our high-quality books,
call toll free 1-800-542-2595 or fax 1-877-542-2596.

Library of Congress Cataloging-in-Publication Data

Ballard, Carol.
How your eyes work / Carol Ballard.
    p. cm. -- (Your body at work)
Includes index.
ISBN 978-1-4339-4109-2 (library binding)
1. Eye--Juvenile literature. 2. Vision--Juvenile literature. I. Title.
QP475.7.B36 2011
612.8'4--dc22
                                2010015860

This edition first published in 2011 by
Gareth Stevens Publishing
111 East 14th Street, Suite 349
New York, NY 10003

Editorial Director: Kerri O'Donnell
Design Director: Haley Harasymiw

Photo Credits:
Chapel Studios 4, 5 (top), 7, 22; Chris Fairclough 13, 21, 28; Gary Fry/RNIB 27; Robert Harding 4,
16; Dmitry Naumov/Shutterstock *cover*; Reflections 17; Tony Stone title page, 19; Zefa contents
page, 5, 18, 20, 23 and 29. The remaining pictures are from the Wayland Picture Library.

Illustrations:
Kevin Jones Associates and Michael Courtney

Printed in the China
CPSIA compliance information: Batch #WAS10GS: For further information contact Gareth Stevens, New York, New York at 1-800-542-2595.

Contents

Eyes   4

Look at Your Eyes   6

Inside an Eye   8

How Do Eyes Work?   10

Light and Dark   12

Near, Far, and Wide   14

Seeing in Color   16

Do You Need Glasses?   18

A Visit to the Optician   20

As You Grow   22

Optical Illusions   24

Blindness   26

Look After Your Eyes   28

Glossary   30

Further Reading   31

Index   32

Eyes

Our eyes are very important. We use them to find out about the world around us.

▲
Would you enjoy your favorite television show if you could not see the screen?

Our eyes help to keep us safe. We use them to look for traffic before we cross the street. We also use them to stop us from bumping into things.

**ALL TRAFFIC
PAY TOLL
1 MILE**

▲
◄ *We use our eyes to watch for warning signs and signals.*

Our eyes allow us to enjoy the world we live in. If we look carefully, we can see tiny animals and plants, beautiful countryside, and wonderful views. In cities, there are interesting buildings that we often walk past without even noticing. This book will tell you more about your eyes and how they work.

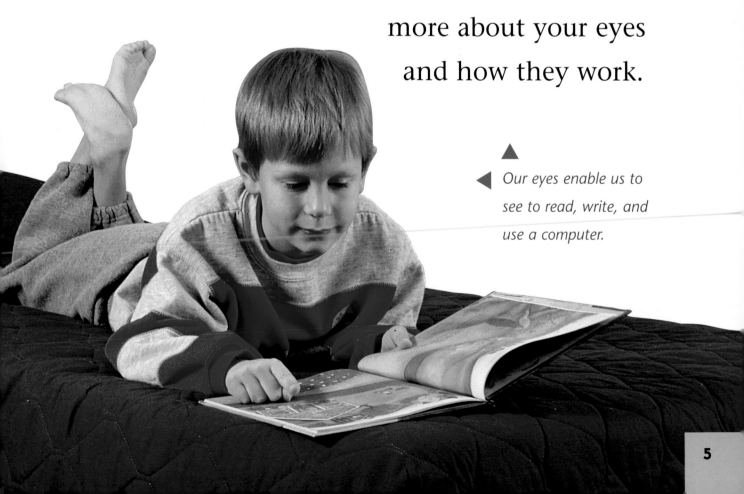

▲
◀ *Our eyes enable us to see to read, write, and use a computer.*

Look at Your Eyes

When you look at your eyes, you can see that they are made up of many parts.

Eyebrows are ridges of skin with short, flat hairs attached. They keep dust and sweat out of the eyes, and protect them against bright sunlight.

▲

A camel's long eyelashes help to protect its eyes from sand and bright sunlight.

Eyelids and eyelashes prevent dust and dirt getting in the eyes. Eyelids keep the eyes moist. When you blink, tear fluid is spread over the surface of your eyes.

◄ *Members of a family often have the same color eyes.*

The white part of the eye is called the **sclera**. At the center of the eye, the sclera is clear so that light can pass through it. This clear part is called the **cornea**.

The colored part of the eye is called the **iris**.
At the center of each eye is a black circle called the **pupil**. This is a hole that lets light into the eye.

The color of the iris depends on the amount of pigment in it. Brown eyes have a lot of pigment, blue eyes have less.

▼

Inside an Eye

Your eye is like a soft, hollow ball filled with liquid and jelly. Inside the eye, the ball is divided into two parts called chambers. The small front chamber is filled with a watery liquid. The other larger chamber is filled with a soft jelly. The jelly and the liquid make the eyes solid and shaped like a ball.

▲
Each eyeball lies inside a bony hollow in the skull. These hollows are strong and protect the eyes from injury.

Between the two chambers is a clear disc called the **lens**. This is held in place by rings of muscles.

At the back of the eye is a layer called the **retina**. The lens bends the light as it enters the eye to **focus** on the retina. The retina reacts when light hits it and sends a message along the **optic nerve** to the brain.

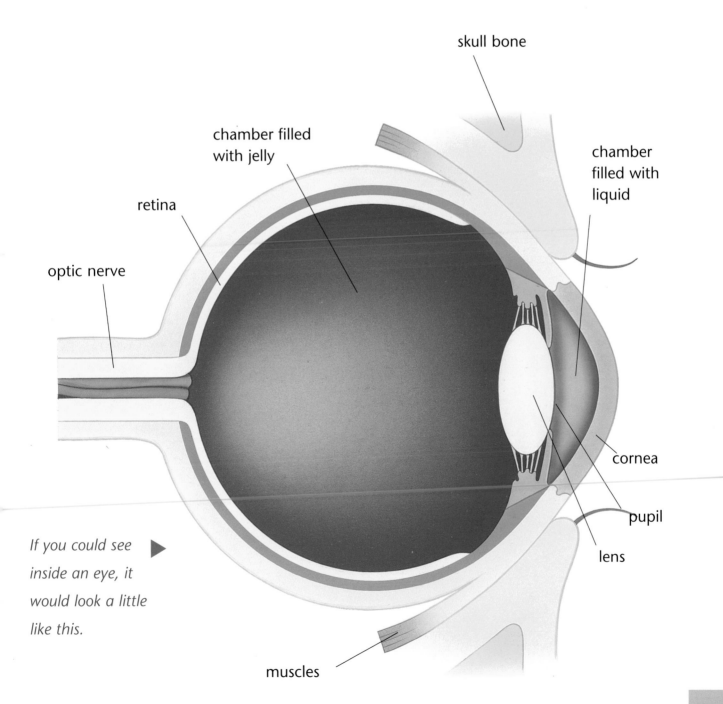

skull bone

chamber filled with jelly

chamber filled with liquid

retina

optic nerve

cornea

pupil

If you could see inside an eye, it would look a little like this.

lens

muscles

How Do Eyes Work?

We need light to be able to see. Imagine you are looking at a tree. Light from the sun falls on the tree. It bounces off the tree and travels to your eyes. Light passes through the cornea, which bends it a little. It then passes through the front chamber and pupil to the lens. As the light rays pass through the lens, they are bent more. They then pass through the back chamber of your eye to the retina.

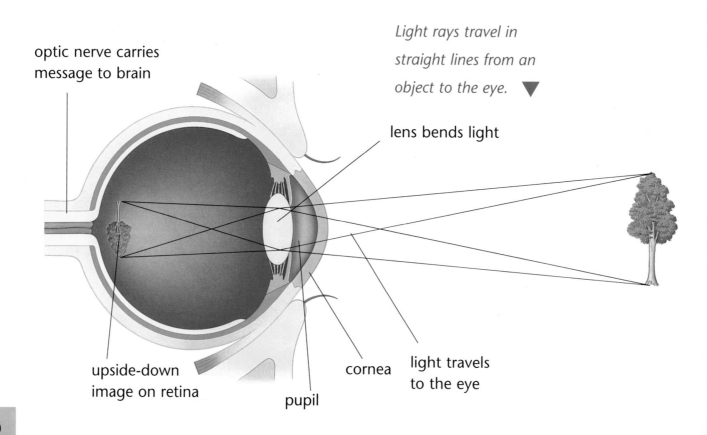

optic nerve carries message to brain

Light rays travel in straight lines from an object to the eye. ▼

lens bends light

upside-down image on retina

pupil

cornea

light travels to the eye

When light lands on the retina, an **image** of the tree is formed. Because the lens bends the light, the image on the retina is upside-down.

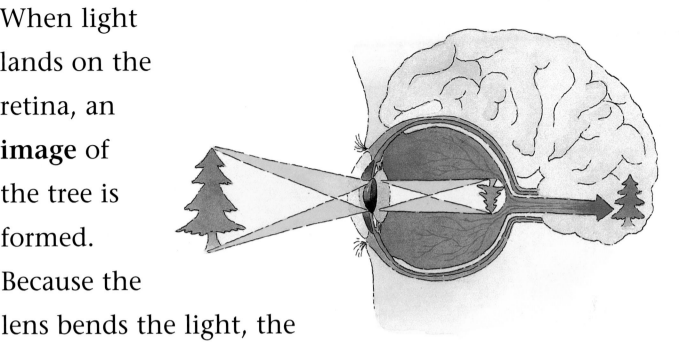

The retinas of both eyes send messages about the tree to the brain. The brain sorts both messages and you "see" the tree. All this happens so quickly that it seems to take no time at all.

Your eye is like a camera. Light passes through a hole and is bent by a lens. A picture is formed at the back of the eye. In a camera, the picture is on a film.

Light and Dark

We can only see clearly if the right amount of light enters our eyes. If the light is too bright, we screw our faces up. This pulls our eyelids closer together and shuts out some of the light.

▲

Cats' eyes have an extra layer inside. This reflects any light that shines on them, so they seem to glow in the dark.

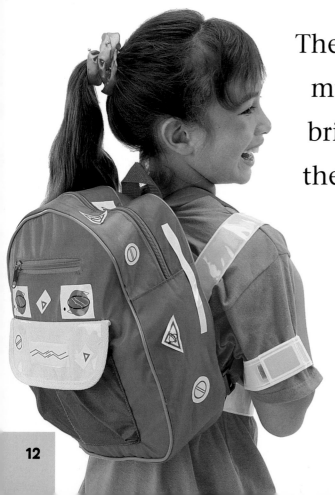

The size of the pupils controls how much light enters the eyes. In bright light, the pupils close until they are just a tiny hole. This keeps out a lot of light. In dim light, the pupils open wide to let in as much light as possible.

◀ *Reflective strips on this girl's backpack will help drivers to see her in the dark.*

Look carefully at your eyes in a mirror. Can you see how big your pupils are? Now shut your eyes and cover them with your hands. Count slowly to one hundred. Open your eyes and look in the mirror right away. How big are your pupils now? Can you explain why they change?

▲
Pupils are large in dim light.

▲
We can see clearly in normal light.

▲
We screw our eyes up in bright light.

Near, Far, and Wide

You can judge distances and shapes because you have two eyes. When you look at something, each eye has a slightly different view of it and sends a different message to your brain. Your brain puts the two messages together and figures out a balanced view.

When you look at a cube like this, your left eye sees more of the red side and your right eye sees more of the green side. The brain puts this information together and you get a balanced view. ▼

To see objects at different distances, each lens has to change its shape. To see near objects, each lens becomes fatter. To see distant objects, each lens becomes thinner.

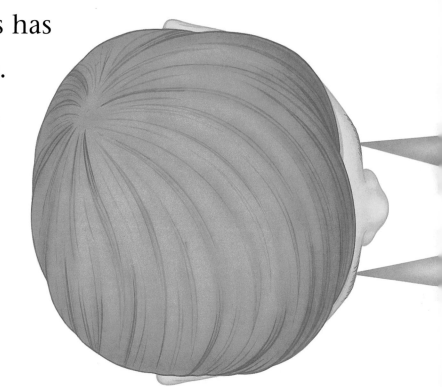

To see things at the side and behind, we have to turn our heads. To find out how far to the side you can see, look straight ahead at something. First, get a friend to stand behind you and then slowly walk around you in a circle. Keep staring straight ahead, and tell your friend to stop when you can see him or her.

▲

A hawk's eyes are at the front of its head so it can find its prey ahead. A rabbit's eyes are on the sides of its head so it has an all-around view of any danger.

Seeing in Color

The retina is made up of millions of **cells**. There are two types of cell in the retina that react to light. These are called rods and cones.

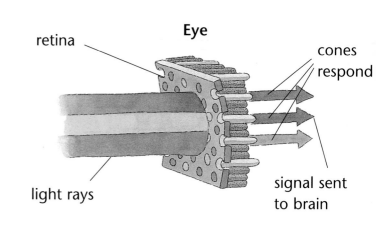

Eye

retina

cones respond

light rays

signal sent to brain

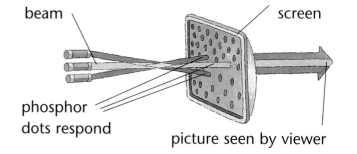

Television

electron beam

television screen

phosphor dots respond

picture seen by viewer

Rods **detect** the amount of light that lands on them. Cones detect the color of the light that lands on them. When you look at a toy, the rods tell the brain how light or dark the toy is. The cones tell the brain what color the toy is.

▲
Each retina is like a living television screen. Electronic receptors in television screens detect red, green, or blue light.

◄ *People who are color blind may not see the numbers among the dots.*

There are three types of cone cell. Each cone cell reacts to just one of the primary colors of light— red, green, or blue. If you look at a red apple, the red cone cells react but the blue and green cone cells do not.

People who cannot see a full range of colors are color blind. To someone who is red-green color blind, a red apple and green grass would look the same color.

This boy is having his eyes tested for color blindness.

Do You Need Glasses?

People wear glasses
for different reasons.
Nearsighted people
can see objects that
are close to them,
but objects far away from them
are blurred. Their glasses help
them to see distant objects
more clearly.

You should be able to read a book easily if you hold it about 12 inches (30 cm) away from your eyes.

Farsighted people can see objects that are far away easily, but find it hard to see things that are close to them. Their glasses help them to see close objects more clearly.

An optician checks to see that this child's eyes are heathy.

Some children can see clearly but need to wear glasses to correct other eye problems. Glasses can sometimes help if a child's eyes do not work together, or if they are not developing properly.

Can you read a book and see the computer screen clearly? If not, you may need glasses. Tell an adult so that an eye test can be planned.
▼

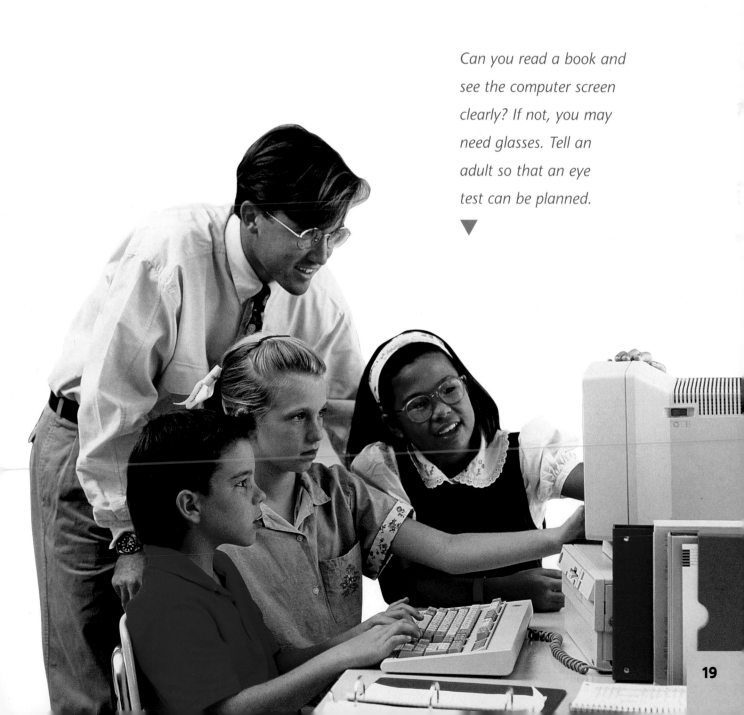

A Visit to the Optician

Katie is going to see the optician to have her eyes tested. To make sure she gets the right glasses, the optician asks her if any of her family wear glasses or have eye problems, and if she is taking any medicines. The optician asks her if she has had any headaches.

Contact lenses are tiny lenses that fit on the front of each eye. They need careful cleaning.

The optician checks that Katie can read the different-sized letters on the chart.

The optician asks Katie to read some letters on a chart. First, she reads with both eyes together. Then the optician covers up each eye one at a time, and she reads the chart with each eye. He shines a light into Katie's eyes to look inside them and check the retina at the back of each eye.

Once the optician has finished all his tests, he knows which lenses Katie needs to help her see clearly.

An optician takes measurements to make sure that this girl's glasses will fit properly.

As You Grow

When they are first born, babies cannot see tiny objects or a lot of detail. After a few months, their eyes can follow a moving toy or person. They do not start to see really clearly until they are a couple of years old.

▲

People often need more than one pair of glasses as they get older, but they only wear one at a time!

Young children may need glasses to help them see. They cannot read letters, and some are too young to talk, so opticians use cards with patterns and pictures to test their eyesight.

◄ *A baby can see movements and shapes but cannot see details clearly.*

Many children start to wear glasses during their first years at school. Some will need to wear them for the rest of their lives. Others will need to wear them for just a few years until the problem is corrected.

As they get older, some people find that they cannot see as well as they did when they were younger. Wearing glasses or contact lenses helps them to see more clearly.

Optical Illusions

Sometimes the brain gets confused about what it sees. These pictures are called optical illusions. Take a look at them. What do you see? Usually, the brain uses information from the eyes and memory to make sense of what you are looking at, but sometimes the brain can get it wrong.

What do you see? Two black faces or one white candlestick? A young girl or an old witch? There are two images in each picture. Your eyes send all the information and your brain has to choose which you see.

A

B

C

▲

Look carefully at these lines. Which do you think is longest, A, B, or C? Now measure them with a ruler. Surprised? The short, outside lines trick your brain. Those on A make the line look longer and those on C make it look shorter.

▲

Put a strip of thin card upright on the dotted line. Look at the bird and the cage. Gradually move your head closer to the page until your nose rests on the card. What happens? Your brain gets a picture of a bird from your left eye and a picture of a cage from your right eye. It has to put the information together so you see the bird inside the cage. (If you don't see the bird inside the cage, try a taller or shorter piece of card.)

Blindness

For **blind** people to lead **independent** lives, they need special help.

A guide dog means that a blind person can go outside safely. Guide dogs are trained to guide their owner around obstacles such as lampposts.

The owner gives the dog instructions by pulling on its special harness.

◄ *A guide dog can help a blind person to move around safely.*

Many blind people read using a special alphabet called **Braille**. A pattern of raised dots stands for each letter, and the person reads it by feeling the dots with their fingers.

There are many objects specially designed to help blind people live a normal life.

Instead of lights and signs, blind people often rely on sound. They can tell the time by using a talking watch. A special clip on the side of a cup bleeps when liquid touches it, so the person knows when the cup is full. Blind people are very neat and tidy. They put things down carefully so they know exactly where things are the next time they want them.

This blind girl is reading a Braille book. The machine in front of her is called a brailler, which she uses to type in Braille.

27

Look After Your Eyes

It is important to look after your eyes, whether or not you wear glasses. Here are some suggestions about how to keep your eyes healthy.

A balanced diet provides the vitamins you need for healthy eyes.

Computer and television screens can be bad for your eyes if you sit in front of them for a long time without a break. When watching the television, try not to sit too close. It can be tempting to hold a book right under your nose when you read, but it is much better to hold it about 12 inches (30 cm) away.

You can get goggles made with your lenses so that you can see more easily in the swimming pool.

28

If you do wear glasses or contact lenses, visit the optician regularly to have your eyes tested. Follow the optician's advice and wear your glasses when you are supposed to. If you play a lot of sports, wearing safety glasses can reduce the risk of an eye injury.

Goggles protect ▶
these children's eyes
from the glare of
the snow.

Glossary

blind Unable to see.

Braille An alphabet of raised dots.

cells The millions of tiny building blocks that make up the body.

cornea The clear covering of the front of the eyeball.

detect To notice or pick up information.

focus To produce a clear image.

glare Bright, strong sunlight.

image A picture made by light.

independent To be able to look after oneself.

iris The colored part of the eye.

lens The clear disc that bends light to focus on the retina.

optic nerve The nerve that carries messages from the eye to the brain.

pigment A substance in the iris that gives it color.

pupil The hole that lets light into the eye.

retina The back layer of the eye that is sensitive to light.

sclera The thick, white covering of most of the eyeball that gives the eye its rounded shape.

Further Reading

Books to Read

Body Focus: Eyes
by Carol Ballard
Heinemann-Raintree, 2009

The Sense of Sight
by Ellen Weiss
Children's Press, 2009

Web Sites

http://kidshealth.org/kid/htbw/eyes.html

http://www.enchantedlearning.com/themes/senses.shtml

Index

blindness 26, 27

blinking 6

Braille 27

brain 9, 11, 14, 16, 24

color 16, 17

color blindness 16–17

cones 16, 17

contact lenses 20, 23, 29

cornea 7, 11

eyebrows 6

eyelashes 6

eyelids 6, 12

eye test 20–21, 22, 29

farsightedness 18

glasses 18, 19, 20, 22,
   23, 28, 29

guide dog 26

iris 7

lens 8, 9, 11, 14

light 7, 9, 10, 11, 12, 16

muscles 8

nearsightedness 18

optic nerve 9

optical illusions 24–25

optician 18, 20, 21, 22, 29

pupil 7, 11, 12, 13

retina 9, 11, 16, 21

rods 16

sclera 7

tear fluid 6